United States Government Accountability Office

GAO

Report to the Chairman, Subcommittee on Oversight of Government Management, the Federal Workforce, and the District of Columbia, Committee on Homeland Security and Governmental Affairs, U.S. Senate

June 2012

DEPARTMENT OF STATE

I0426217

Foreign Service Midlevel Staffing Gaps Persist Despite Significant Increases in Hiring

GAO

Accountability ★ Integrity ★ Reliability

GAO-12-721

G A O
Accountability * Integrity * Reliability

Highlights

Highlights of GAO-12-721, a report to the Chairman, Subcommittee on Oversight of Government Management, the Federal Workforce, and the District of Columbia, Committee on Homeland Security and Governmental Affairs, U.S. Senate

DEPARTMENT OF STATE

Foreign Service Midlevel Staffing Gaps Persist Despite Significant Increases in Hiring

Why GAO Did This Study

In 2009, GAO reported on challenges that State faced in filling its increasing overseas staffing needs with sufficiently experienced personnel and noted that persistent Foreign Service staffing and experience gaps put diplomatic readiness at risk. State is currently undertaking a new hiring plan, known as "Diplomacy 3.0," to increase the size of the Foreign Service by 25 percent to close staffing gaps and respond to new diplomatic priorities. However, fiscal constraints are likely to delay the plan's full implementation well beyond its intended target for completion in 2013. In addition, State's first Quadrennial Diplomacy and Development Review highlighted the need to find ways to close overseas gaps. GAO was asked to assess (1) the extent to which State's overseas midlevel experience gaps in the Foreign Service have changed since 2008 and (2) State's efforts to address these gaps. GAO analyzed State's personnel data; reviewed key planning documents, including the Five Year Workforce Plan; and interviewed State officials in Washington, D.C., and at selected posts.

What GAO Recommends

GAO recommends that State update its Five Year Workforce Plan to include a strategy to address midlevel Foreign Service gaps and a plan to evaluate the success of this strategy. State reviewed a draft of this report and agreed with GAO's recommendation.

View GAO-12-721. For more information, contact Michael Courts at (202) 512-8980 or courtsm@gao.gov.

What GAO Found

The Department of State (State) faces persistent experience gaps in overseas Foreign Service positions, particularly at the midlevels, and these gaps have not diminished since 2008. In fiscal years 2009 and 2010, State increased the size of the Foreign Service by 17 percent. However, these new hires will not have the experience to reach midlevels until fiscal years 2014 and 2015. As shown in the figure, GAO found that 28 percent of overseas Foreign Service positions were either vacant or filled by upstretch candidates—officers serving in positions above their grade—as of October 2011, a percentage that has not changed since 2008. Midlevel positions represent the largest share of these gaps. According to State officials, the gaps have not diminished because State increased the total number of overseas positions in response to increased needs and emerging priorities. State officials noted the department takes special measures to fill high-priority positions, including those in Afghanistan, Iraq, and Pakistan.

Overseas Foreign Service Positions Filled at Grade, Filled with Upstretch Assignments, and Vacant, 2008 and 2011

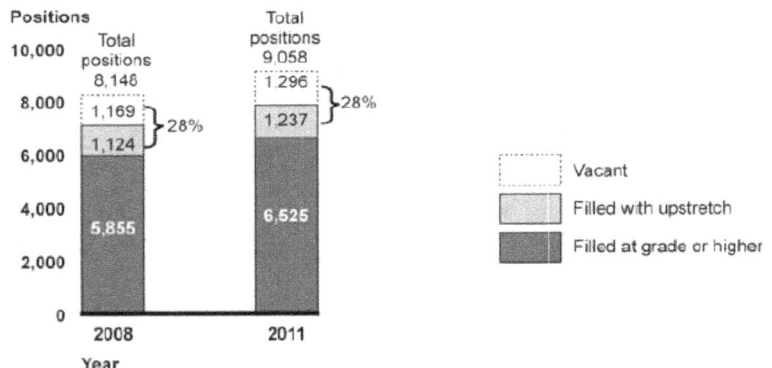

Source: GAO analysis of State data.

State has taken steps to increase its reliance on Civil Service employees and retirees, as well as expand mentoring, to help address midlevel experience gaps overseas; however, State lacks a strategy to guide these efforts. State is currently implementing a pilot program to expand overseas assignments for Civil Service employees. Efforts to expand the limited number of these assignments must overcome some key challenges, such as addressing new gaps when Civil Service employees leave their headquarters positions and identifying qualified Civil Service applicants to fill overseas vacancies. State also hires retirees on a limited basis for both full-time and short-term positions. For example, State used limited congressional authority to offer dual compensation waivers to hire 57 retirees in 2011. As a step toward mitigating experience gaps overseas, State began a pilot program offering workshops that include mentoring for first-time supervisors. State acknowledges the need to close midlevel Foreign Service gaps, but it has not developed a strategy to help ensure that the department is taking full advantage of available human capital flexibilities and evaluating the success of its efforts to address these gaps.

_____ **United States Government Accountability Office**

Contents

Figures

Abbreviations

AFSA	American Foreign Service Association
AIP countries	Afghanistan, Iraq, and Pakistan
BSRP	Bureau Strategic and Resource Plan
GEMS	Global Employee Management System
LNA	Limited Non-Career Appointment
OMS	Office Management Specialist
QDDR	Quadrennial Diplomacy and Development Review
State	Department of State
WAE	When Actually Employed

June 14, 2012

The Honorable Daniel Akaka
Chairman
Subcommittee on Oversight of Government
    Management, the Federal Workforce,
    and the District of Columbia
Committee on Homeland Security
    and Governmental Affairs
United States Senate

Dear Mr. Chairman:

The Department of State (State) staffs U.S. Foreign Service employees to more than 270 posts worldwide to carry out American foreign policy. In 2009, we reported on challenges that State faced in filling its increasing overseas staffing needs with sufficiently experienced personnel and noted that persistent Foreign Service staffing and experience gaps put diplomatic readiness at risk.[1] State has acknowledged that the priority it places on meeting huge staffing demands in Afghanistan, Iraq, and Pakistan—referred to as AIP countries—has contributed to gaps elsewhere, despite efforts to hire Foreign Service employees at levels above attrition. State is currently undertaking a new hiring plan, known as "Diplomacy 3.0," to increase the size of the Foreign Service by 25 percent to close staffing gaps and respond to new diplomatic priorities. However, fiscal constraints are likely to delay full implementation of this increase well beyond its intended target for completion in 2013. State also recognizes that it will take a number of years before entry-level officers hired under Diplomacy 3.0 gain the experience needed to fill the shortfall in midlevel positions. State's first Quadrennial Diplomacy and Development Review (QDDR), released in 2010, highlighted the need to find additional ways to close overseas experience gaps at the midlevels, including drawing on the expertise of the department's Civil Service employees and Foreign Service retirees, and expanding mentoring programs.

---

[1]GAO, *Department of State: Additional Steps Needed to Address Continuing Staffing and Experience Gaps at Hardship Posts*, GAO-09-874 (Washington, D.C.: Sept. 17, 2009).

In response to your request, we assessed (1) the extent to which State's overseas midlevel experience gaps in the Foreign Service have changed since 2008 and (2) State's efforts to address these gaps.

To address these objectives, we analyzed State's personnel data from the department's Global Employee Management System (GEMS), as of September 2008 and October 2011. We did not validate whether the total number of authorized overseas positions was appropriate or met State's needs. We also analyzed State data on the use of retirees and Civil Service employees in overseas posts; key planning documents, including State's Five Year Workforce and Leadership Succession Plan, the QDDR, the Bureau of Human Resources' Strategic and Resource Plan, and other relevant documents; and our previous reports on human capital challenges at State and effective strategic workforce planning at other federal agencies. We also interviewed State officials at the Bureau of Human Resources, as well as the Bureau of Consular Affairs and the six regional bureaus; the American Foreign Service Association (AFSA); and the American Academy of Diplomacy. In addition, we interviewed management officers at selected overseas posts. Appendix I contains a more detailed description of our scope and methodology.

We conducted this performance audit from June 2011 to June 2012 in accordance with generally accepted government auditing standards. Those standards require that we plan and perform the audit to obtain sufficient, appropriate evidence to provide a reasonable basis for our findings and conclusions based on our audit objectives. We believe that the evidence obtained provides a reasonable basis for our findings and conclusions based on our audit objectives.

Background

State is the lead agency responsible for implementing American foreign policy and representing the United States abroad. It staffs over 270 embassies, consulates, and other posts worldwide. Figure 1 shows the number and share of State's Foreign Service, Civil Service, and Locally Employed staff. According to State, about two-thirds of the Foreign Service serves overseas at a given point in time, whereas almost all Civil

Service employees serve domestically.[2] Locally Employed staff serve overseas.[3]

Figure 1: State's Workforce by Employee Type, as of June 30, 2011

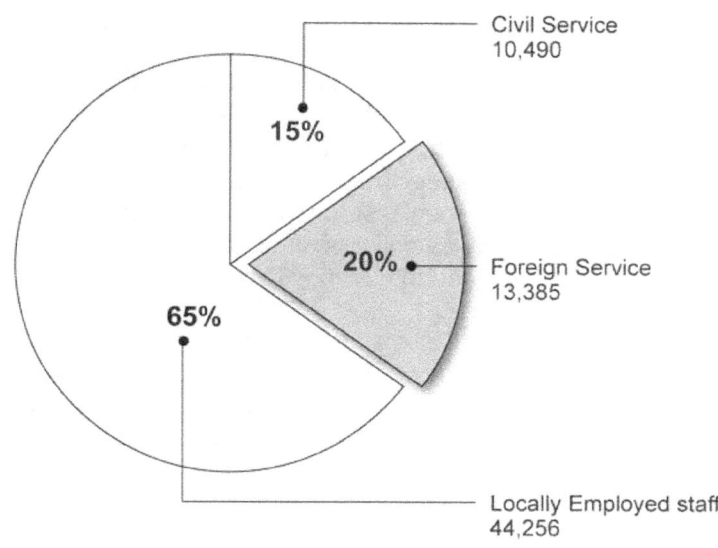

Civil Service
10,490

15%

20% Foreign Service
13,385

65%

Locally Employed staff
44,256

Source: GAO analysis of State data.

Foreign Service Workforce

Foreign Service employees serving abroad fall into two broad categories—generalists and specialists. Generalists help formulate and implement the foreign policy of the United States and are grouped into five career tracks: consular, economic, management, political, and public diplomacy. Specialists serve in 18 different skill groups to support overseas posts worldwide or in Washington, D.C. These skill groups are grouped into eight major categories: Administration, Construction Engineering, Facility Management, Information Technology, International

---

[2]Civil Service employees work in a variety of areas at State domestically, including Budget Administration, Contract Procurement, Foreign Affairs, General Accounting and Administration, Information Technology Management, Legal Counsel, Management Analysis, Passport Visa Services, Personnel Management, and Public Affairs.

[3]Locally Employed staff include foreign nationals and U.S. citizen residents employed via direct-hire appointments, personal services agreements, and personal services contracts.

Information and English Language Programs, Medical and Health, Office Management, and Security.

State typically hires Foreign Service employees at the entry level. Among Foreign Service generalists, the entry-level consists of three position grades—06, 05, and 04.[4] Midlevel positions include grades 03, 02, and 01, and senior-level positions include career minister, minister counselor, and counselor positions. Officers compete annually for promotion to the next higher grade. It typically takes about 4 to 5 years for an officer to move through the entry-level grades to a midlevel grade. The levels associated with Foreign Service specialist position grades vary across specialist function. For example, a senior-level office management specialist position is a 04 grade, whereas a senior-level medical technician position is a 02 grade.

State requires its Foreign Service employees to be available for service anywhere in the world and reserves the ability to direct officers to any of its posts overseas or to its Washington headquarters. However, the department does not generally use this authority, preferring other means of filling high-priority positions, according to State officials. The process of assigning Foreign Service employees to their positions typically begins when they receive a list of upcoming vacancies for which they may compete. Foreign Service employees then submit a list of positions for which they want to be considered, or "bids," to the Office of Career Development and Assignments and consult with their career development officer. The process varies depending on an officer's grade and functional specialty, and State uses a variety of incentives to encourage Foreign Service employees to bid on hardship posts, including the high-priority posts in AIP countries.

Five Year Workforce Plan

State has a Five Year Workforce Plan, which it updates annually. This document describes State's strategic workforce planning process, which includes the following five elements:

- *Establish strategic alignment*: links human resources to strategic goals.

---

[4]Within the Foreign Service, grade numbers decrease as a position's level rises.

- *Identify gaps by analysis of requirements and talent pool:* compares estimated staffing requirements to projected workforce levels to identify workforce gaps and strength.

- *Develop management plans:* develop plans related to recruitment, hiring, promotion, training, and career development.

- *Implement management plans:* implement plans related to recruitment, hiring, promotion, training, and career development.

- *Evaluate strategies:* evaluate plans, strategies, programs, and initiatives.

Overseas Staffing Model

State uses an Overseas Staffing Model, which it updates every 2 years, to ensure that the department's personnel resources are aligned with its strategic priorities and foreign policy objectives. The model uses a variety of inputs—such as the priority level of overseas posts, visa processing requirements, and security needs—to estimate the required Foreign Service staffing levels at each overseas location. The model includes seven categories of embassies based primarily on the level and type of work required to pursue the U.S. government's diplomatic relations with the host country. For example, the lowest-level category includes special-purpose small embassies with limited requirements for advocacy, liaison, and coordination in the host country's capital. The highest-level category includes the largest, most comprehensive full-service posts where the host country's regional and global role requires extensive U.S. personnel resources.

Recent Hiring Initiatives

State has sought to rebuild the size of its Foreign Service after a period of hiring below attrition levels during the 1990s that contributed to staffing gaps overseas and endangered diplomatic readiness, according to the department. To address these gaps, State implemented the "Diplomatic Readiness Initiative," which resulted in hiring over 1,000 new employees above attrition from 2002 to 2004. However, as we previously reported, most of this increase was absorbed by the demand for personnel in Afghanistan and Iraq.[5] In 2009, State began another hiring effort called

---

[5]GAO, *Department of State: Staffing and Foreign Language Shortfalls Persist Despite Initiatives to Address Gaps*, GAO-06-894 (Washington, D.C.: Aug. 4, 2006).

Diplomacy 3.0 to increase its Foreign Service workforce by 25 percent by 2013. However, due to emerging budgetary constraints, State now anticipates this goal will not be met until 2023.

Findings from 2009 GAO Report on Staffing Hardship Posts

In 2009, we reported that State faced persistent staffing and experience gaps at overseas posts, particularly at the midlevel.[6] The report's analysis of State's personnel data, as of September 2008, found that posts with the greatest hardship levels had higher vacancy rates than posts with no or low hardship levels.[7] Posts with the greatest hardship also were more likely to fill positions through "upstretch" assignments—assignments in which the position's grade is at least one grade higher than that of the officer assigned to it. The report also found that these staffing and experience gaps can compromise posts' diplomatic readiness in a variety of ways. For example, gaps can lead to decreased reporting coverage; loss of institutional knowledge; and increased supervisory requirements for senior staff, detracting from other critical diplomatic responsibilities.

In addition, we reported on a variety of measures and incentives that State used to help ensure that Foreign Service employees bid on hardship posts. These ranged from monetary benefits to changes in service and bidding requirements. In response to our recommendation, State evaluated these measures and incentives in 2011. According to State officials, this evaluation found that officers used the entire range of incentives available—financial and nonfinancial—based on preferences and priorities and that career stage and family status were key to affecting the officers' decisions.

---

[6]GAO-09-874.

[7]State defines hardship posts as those locations where the U.S. government provides differential pay incentives—an additional 5 percent to 35 percent of basic salary, depending on the severity or difficulty of the conditions—to encourage employees to bid on assignments to these posts and to compensate employees for the hardships they encounter. For the purposes of this report, we refer to these differential pay incentives as hardship differentials. We define hardship posts as those posts where the hardship differential is at least 15 percent. We define posts of greatest hardship as those where the hardship differential is at least 25 percent. We define posts with low hardship differentials as those where the hardship differential is 5 percent or 10 percent. We define posts with no hardship differentials as those where the hardship differential is 0 percent.

Even with Increased Hiring, State Faces Persistent Midlevel Experience Gaps Overseas

State increased the size of the Foreign Service by about 17 percent in fiscal years 2009 and 2010, but overseas experience gaps—the percentage of positions that are vacant or filled with upstretch assignments—have not declined since 2008 because State increased the total number of overseas positions in response to increased needs and emerging diplomatic priorities. These gaps are largest at the midlevels and in hardship posts. According to State officials, the department takes special measures to fill high-priority positions.

State Increased Hiring under Diplomacy 3.0 but Revised Its Targets for Future Years

State made substantial progress in fiscal years 2009 and 2010 toward the Diplomacy 3.0 goal of increasing the size of the Foreign Service by 25 percent by 2013. In those years, State hired about 1,900 Foreign Service employees above attrition, increasing the total size of the Foreign Service by about 17 percent, or over two-thirds of its total 5-year goal. According to State, in addition to expanding overseas staffing, the increase in hiring allowed the department to double the size of the training complement, which provides flexibility to enroll Foreign Service employees in language courses—some of which require up to 2 years of training—without increasing the size of overseas gaps.

However, due to budget constraints, hiring has slowed significantly, and State only added 38 new Foreign Service positions above attrition in fiscal year 2011. In that year, it also modified its hiring projections to reflect a downward revision of future budget estimates for fiscal year 2012 and beyond. State now projects it will add 150 new Foreign Service positions above attrition in fiscal year 2012 and 82 new Foreign Service positions above attrition in each of the following 6 years. As a result, State revised its estimate for when it will complete the Diplomacy 3.0 hiring initiative. In April 2011, State estimated it would complete the increased hiring called for in Diplomacy 3.0 in fiscal year 2018; however, State now estimates it will not complete the hiring initiative until fiscal year 2023. State officials noted that these estimates may be revised again based on future budget environments.

Experience Gaps at Overseas Posts Have Not Declined

Our analysis of State staffing data shows that State faces experience gaps in over one-quarter of Foreign Service positions at overseas posts, a proportion that has not changed since 2008. The largest gaps are in midlevel positions, while hardship posts and some position categories, such as Office Management Specialist positions, also have large gaps.

Vacancy and Upstretch Rates Are Unchanged Since 2008

According to our analysis of State staffing data as of October 31, 2011, State faces experience gaps in 28 percent of overseas Foreign Service positions. Specifically, 14 percent of overseas Foreign Service positions are vacant and an additional 14 percent of positions are filled through upstretch assignments.[8] Both percentages, as well as the total percentage of positions facing experience gaps, are unchanged since 2008.

Our analysis indicates that State has not met its goal for reducing the overseas vacancy rate. In its fiscal year 2013 Bureau Strategic and Resource Plan (BSRP), State's Bureau of Human Resources established a goal of reducing the vacancy rate for overseas positions to 8 percent by the end of fiscal year 2011. However, we found that State had an overseas vacancy rate of 14 percent 1 month after the end of that fiscal year.[9] Further, our comparison of data from 2008 and 2011 shows that, while the number of officers serving overseas increased following the Diplomacy 3.0 hiring surge, the number of authorized positions overseas has also increased. Consequently, the overall vacancy rates have not declined. In 2008, approximately 7,000 of about 8,100 total Foreign Service positions were filled. Comparatively, in 2011, nearly 7,800 Foreign Service positions were filled—or 11 percent more positions than in 2008—but the total number of positions increased to over 9,000, resulting in the same vacancy rate.

The overall proportion of overseas positions filled by upstretch assignments is also essentially unchanged since 2008, with approximately 14 percent of all positions assigned to officers with grades below the position's designated grade. State officials noted that some of these upstretch assignments are in midlevel positions that were temporarily downgraded—or ceded—to a lower grade, so that they could be filled by entry-level officers. According to State officials, the work requirements of ceded positions are revised to make the positions more appropriate for an entry-level officer and the department provides training and mentoring to help prepare officers for the position. Therefore, State

---

[8]In filling positions, State does not count any assignments within entry-level positions as upstretch assignments. However, for the purposes of our analysis, we defined an upstretch assignment as any assignment in which the grade of the position is higher than the grade of the incumbent.

[9]The BSRP also set overseas vacancy rate targets of 10 percent in 2010 and 6 percent in 2012. The BSRP stated that the department did not meet its 2010 target with an actual vacancy rate of 16.7 percent.

does not consider an entry-level officer in a ceded position to be in an upstretch assignment.[10] However, officials at overseas posts and in regional bureaus noted that these positions may still suffer from experience gaps. Figure 2 shows that the number of authorized positions and Foreign Service employees serving overseas has increased, but the proportion of positions with experience gaps has not changed.

Figure 2: Overseas Foreign Service Positions Filled at Grade, Filled with Upstretch Assignments, and Vacant, 2008 and 2011

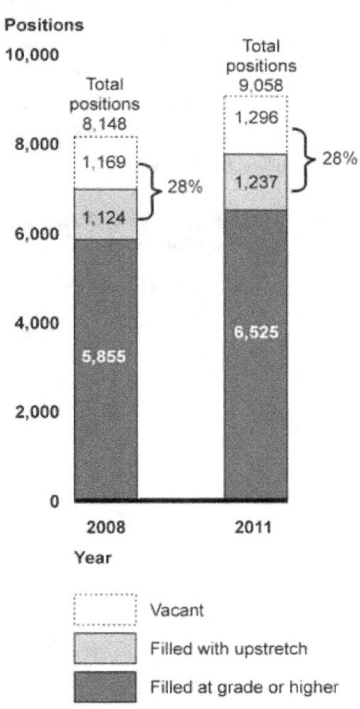

Source: GAO analysis of State data.

State officials noted that AIP posts—State's highest-priority posts—account for much of the increase in new positions. As figure 3 shows, regionally, the largest share of new positions is in the Bureau of South and Central Asian Affairs, primarily because of increases in Afghanistan and Pakistan, and

---

[10]In State's staffing data, ceded positions appear at their original grade and, therefore, we were unable to differentiate entry-level assignments to ceded positions from upstretch assignments.

the majority of new positions are in a small number of countries where State has high levels of engagement. Specifically, about 40 percent of all new positions are in AIP countries and an additional 20 percent are in 5 other countries: Mexico, Brazil, China, India, and Russia. State officials noted that this distribution of new positions reflects the department's changing foreign policy priorities. For example, positions were added in Brazil and China in response to presidential directives to expand consular capacity in those countries. According to State officials, the department has also created positions to address emerging diplomatic priorities, such as climate change and global health. Additionally, State officials noted that most Foreign Service employees hired in fiscal year 2010 would not have been placed in overseas assignments as of October 31, 2011, when we acquired staffing data. State anticipates that overall vacancy rates will drop to approximately 9 percent as officers hired in recent years are fully deployed by the end of 2012.

Figure 3: Locations of Overseas Positions 2008 and 2011, as of October 31, 2011

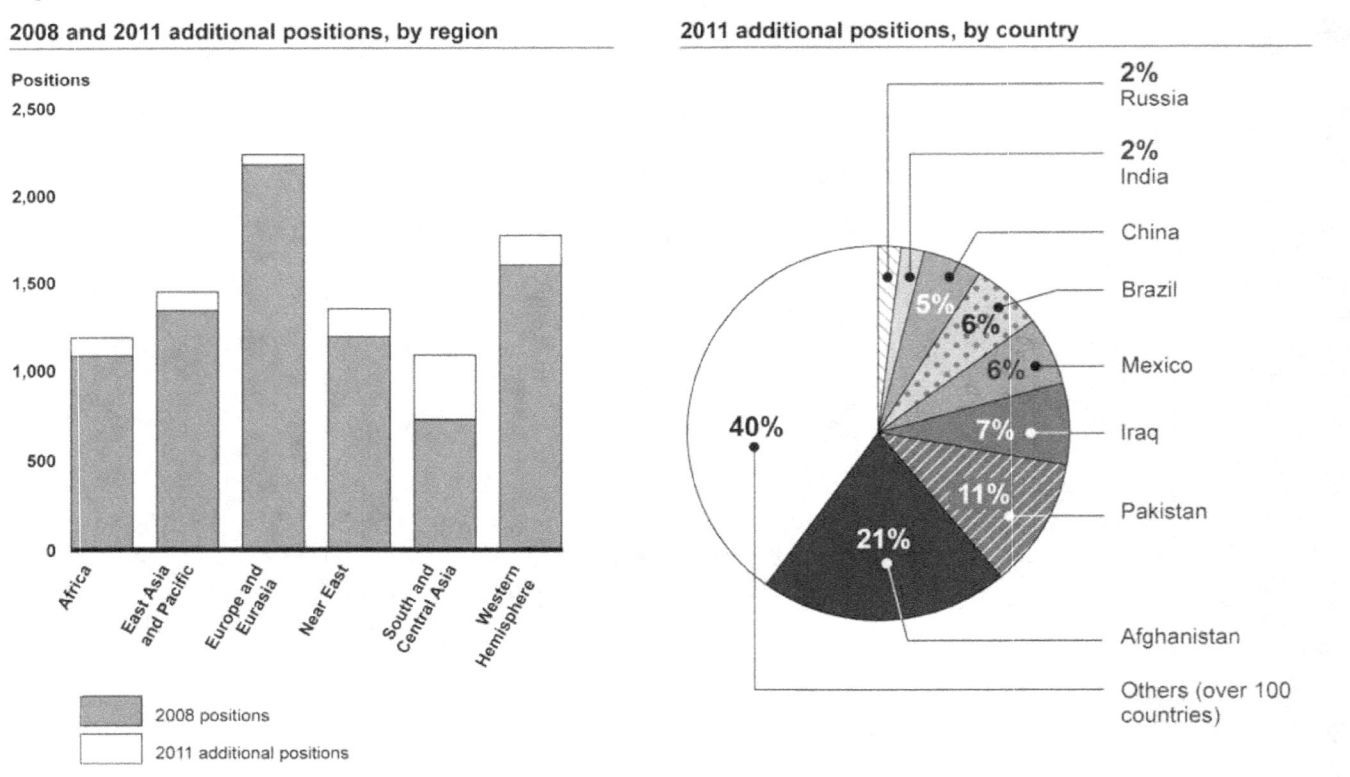

2008 and 2011 additional positions, by region

2011 additional positions, by country

Source: GAO analysis of State data.

GAO-12-721 Foreign Service Workforce Gaps

Midlevel Gaps Persist

Although State intended to eliminate gaps in midlevel Foreign Service positions by the end of fiscal year 2012, these gaps have only diminished slightly since 2008. Specifically, experience gaps currently exist in about 26 percent of midlevel Foreign Service positions—only 2 percent lower than in 2008. About 60 percent of all vacancies and upstretch assignments are in midlevel positions because they make up the largest share of all overseas positions. Figure 4 shows the numbers and percentages of positions filled at grade, filled with upstretch assignments, and vacant for the various position levels.

Figure 4: Position Levels Filled at Grade, Filled with Upstretch Assignments, and Vacant, as of October 31, 2011

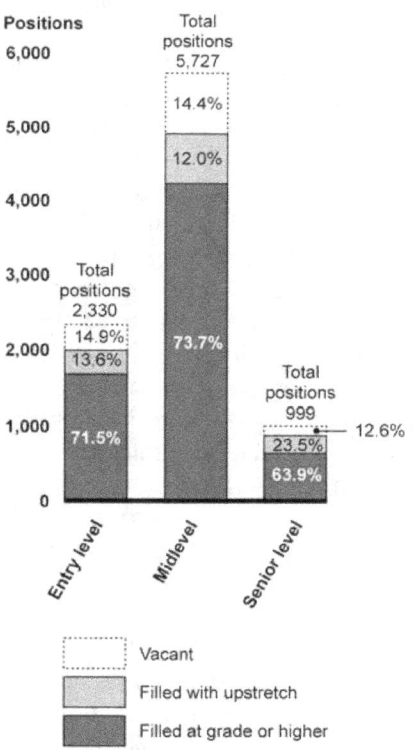

Source: GAO analysis of State data.

Notes: Numbers may not add to 100 percent, due to rounding. According to State officials, senior-level upstretch assignments may be overstated because promotions of officers into the senor levels might not have taken effect as of October 31, 2011.

State has acknowledged that midlevel gaps are a persistent problem. State has faced midlevel gaps for years and, according to the August

2011 Five Year Workforce Plan, the midlevel gap grew from 2010 to 2011. According to State officials, midlevel gaps have grown in recent years because most of the new positions created under Diplomacy 3.0 were midlevel positions and State only hires entry-level Foreign Service employees. In prior reports, we found that midlevel experience gaps compromise diplomatic readiness, and State officials confirmed that these gaps continue to impact overseas operations.

State officials noted that midlevel gaps will decrease as recent hires are promoted. According to State's Five Year Workforce Plan, officers hired in fiscal years 2009 and 2010 under the first wave of Diplomacy 3.0 hiring will begin to be eligible for promotion to the midlevels in fiscal years 2014 or 2015. In recent years, State has accelerated the average time it takes for officers to be promoted into the midlevels, in part to fill gaps. However, officials from State's regional bureaus and AFSA expressed concerns that this creates a different form of experience gap, as some officers may be promoted before they are fully prepared to assume new responsibilities.

A Post's Hardship Level Continues to Be One of the Most Significant Factors Affecting Gaps

Our analysis shows that a post's hardship level continues to be one of the most significant factors for predicting whether a position is filled, remains vacant, or is filled with an upstretch assignment. We found that over 35 percent of all positions in posts of greatest hardship are vacant or filled with upstretch assignments compared to about 22 percent for posts with low or no hardship differentials. Further, our analysis of the likelihood of positions being vacant or filled with an upstretch assignment shows that—controlling for other factors, such as a position's level, type, or regional location—a post's hardship level is one of the most consistent factors for predicting where experience gaps will occur. Specifically, we found that positions in posts of greatest hardship are 44 percent more likely to be vacant than positions at posts with low or no hardship differentials. Additionally, when positions are filled, posts of greatest hardship are 81 percent more likely to use an upstretch candidate than posts with low or no hardship differentials. This is consistent with our findings in prior work, which found that hardship posts faced larger gaps than posts with low or no hardship differential.[11] Appendix II describes our analysis of the likelihood of various positions being vacant or filled with an upstretch assignment in further detail.

[11] See GAO-09-874.

Generalist and Specialist Positions Are Filled at Roughly Equal Rates, but Some Position Categories Are More Difficult to Fill

We found no significant difference between the rates at which generalist and specialist positions are filled. However, the likelihood of generalist positions being filled with upstretch assignments is somewhat higher than for specialist positions. We also found that there are differences in vacancy and upstretch rates for specific functions within both the generalist and specialist fields and that some position categories are more difficult to fill.

Among generalists, the consular section has the largest gaps, in terms of the total number of positions that are vacant or filled with upstretch assignments, because it is the largest generalist section. According to our analysis, about 170 consular positions were vacant as of October 31, 2011, and about 250 consular positions were filled with upstretch assignments. State officials noted that demand is high for entry-level consular officers to adjudicate visas, particularly in countries that have seen dramatic increases in demand for visas in recent years.[12] In addition, the Public Diplomacy section has a relatively high upstretch rate, with nearly one-quarter of all Public Diplomacy positions filled with upstretch assignments. State officials noted that gaps within the Public Diplomacy section, particularly at the midlevels, have persisted since the late 1990s, when the U.S. Information Agency—which had responsibility for public diplomacy—was integrated into State. Figure 5 shows the proportion of positions that are filled at grade or better, filled with upstretch assignments, or are vacant for generalist positions.

---

[12]To help address this gap, State recently introduced a pilot program in Brazil and China to fill entry-level consular positions with non-Foreign Service employees hired on a limited 5-year term.

Figure 5: Generalist Positions Filled at Grade, Filled with Upstretch Assignments, and Vacant, as of October 31, 2011

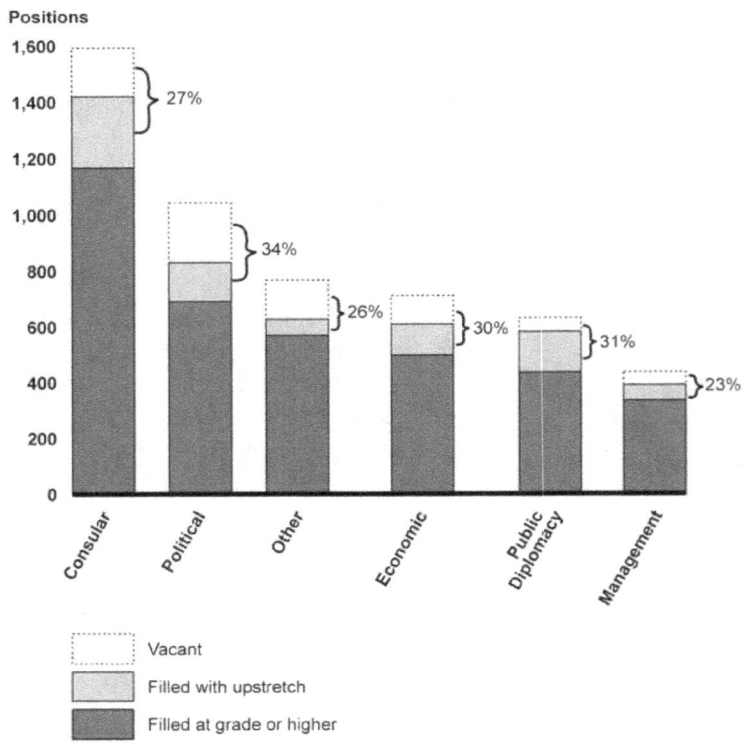

Source: GAO analysis of State data.

Note: "Other" includes positions designated as "Executive" or "International Relations" which, according to State officials, may be filled by officers from any generalist discipline.

Within specialist skill groups, Office Management Specialist (OMS) positions have the largest overall gaps, both in terms of the number of positions and the relative percentage of the gap. Over one-third of all OMS positions, or nearly 300 positions, are either vacant or filled with upstretch assignments. Regional bureau and post officials cited OMS positions as being among the most difficult to fill. For example, officials in Brazil noted that both the embassy in Brasilia and the consulate in Sao Paulo had OMS positions that were vacant for 2 years. Security specialist skill groups also face substantial gaps. The Security Technician and Security Engineer fields have fewer positions than some of the larger specialist fields, but about 30 percent of positions in both fields are vacant or filled with upstretch assignments. Further, security officers have one of the highest vacancy rates among specialist fields, with about 17 percent of those positions unfilled. Figure 6 shows the proportion of positions that are filled at grade, filled with upstretch assignments, or vacant for the 10 largest specialist skill groups.

Figure 6: Positions within the 10 Largest Specialist Skill Groups That Are Filled at Grade, Filled with Upstretch Assignments, and Vacant, as of October 31, 2011

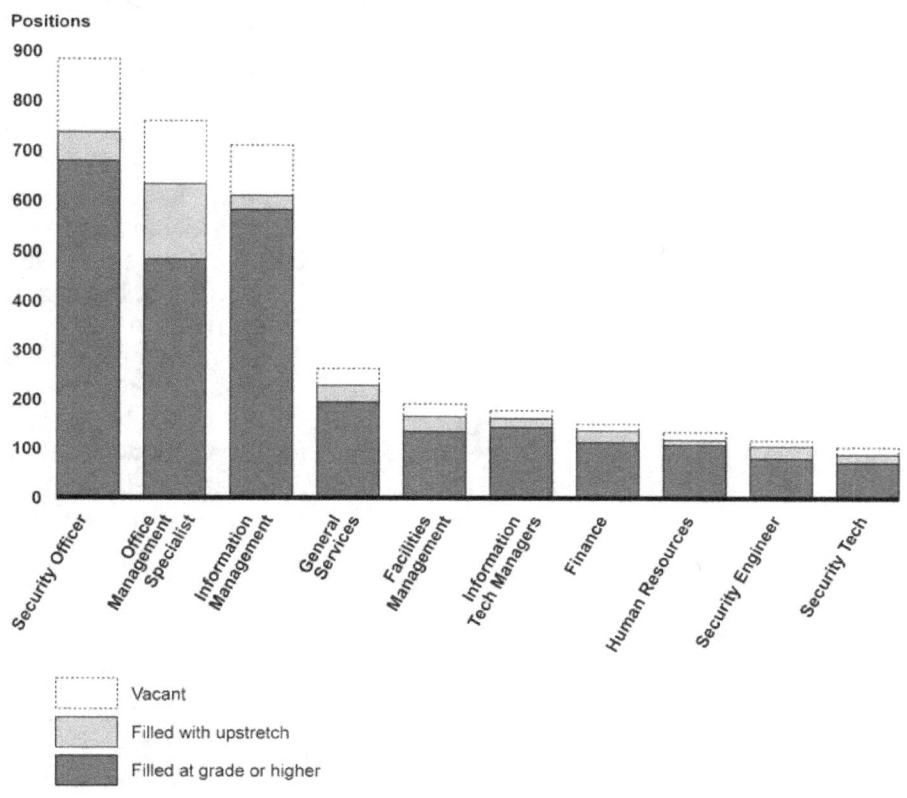

Source: GAO analysis of State data.

Note: In total, there are 18 specialist skill groups, many of which are small. We only show the 10 largest specialist skill groups.

State Takes Special Measures to Fill High-Priority Positions

According to State officials, the department takes a number of steps to help fill high-priority positions. State staggers the assignments process over several months and seeks bids for high-priority areas—including Chiefs of Mission, Deputy Chiefs of Mission, and positions in AIP—before the regular bid cycle. Officials noted that in the most recent cycle for assignments starting in the summer of 2012, State filled about three-quarters of all positions in AIP posts before the regular bid round began.

Regional bureau officials noted that this should have a positive effect on staffing elsewhere because it limits the number of people pulled from other assignments. State continues to fill AIP positions year-round and often uses people from other posts on temporary assignments in AIP posts. According to State, as of February 2012, approximately 91 percent of AIP positions were filled.[13] State also holds an "urgent vacancies" bid round in the spring to fill positions that were not filled in earlier cycles.

State uses a decentralized process for prioritizing and filling overseas positions, which officials stated helps ensure important positions are filled. While AIP posts are the only official department priority for staffing, State officials said regional bureaus informally set their own priorities by determining which of the positions within the bureau that are up for bid are most critical and actively recruiting candidates for those positions. Officials from State's Office of Career Development and Assignments stated that the regional bureaus are in the best position to assess the needs across posts and prioritize positions accordingly. Regional bureau officials stated that, in order to minimize the impact of experience gaps, they will consider factors such as the size of the post or the availability of upper-level support in addition to the needs of the position itself when determining whether a position can remain vacant or be filled through an upstretch assignment. For example, officials stated they may prefer to fill a single position in a small, difficult-to-fill post ahead of multiple positions in a much larger post. Similarly, they may be more likely to allow an upstretch assignment for a lower midlevel position in a large post because larger posts are likely to have more layers of upper management support.

As we reported in 2009, State has created a wide range of measures and financial and nonfinancial incentives to encourage officers to bid on assignments at hardship posts. For example, Foreign Service employees may receive favorable consideration for promotion for service in hardship posts. Additionally, State uses Fair Share bidding rules, which require employees who have not served in a hardship location within the last 8

---

[13]This calculation includes all positions except those that are assigned outside of the regular recruitment and assignments process. State officials noted that a fill rate of 91 percent in AIP does not necessarily indicate that State has been unable to find bidders for 9 percent of AIP positions. For example, State has not sought bids for some positions that are reported as vacant because they are being considered for elimination. In addition, officials noted staffing data are unlikely to show fill rates of 100 percent at any given time because positions are routinely added and removed due to changing needs of the Missions.

years to bid on at least three positions in hardship posts. Officials in the bureaus of Near Eastern Affairs and South and Central Asian Affairs stated that they regularly collect feedback on the impact of incentives in encouraging officers to bid on positions in AIP posts. One official noted that, in addition to financial incentives, nonfinancial incentives, such as additional opportunities or the feeling that they are doing something important, often help to attract bidders. According to State officials, through this system of incentives and bidding rules, State has always been able to find volunteers to fill critical needs. While the department has the authority to direct Foreign Service employees to specific assignments if it does not have adequate bidders for a position, according to State officials, the department has not used these directed assignments— outside of assigning Foreign Service employees in their first or second rotation. State officials noted that use of directed assignments could potentially result in a less motivated or productive workforce.

State Has Taken Steps to Address Midlevel Experience Gaps Overseas but Has Not Included These Steps in Its Workforce Plan

State has taken steps to implement goals highlighted in the QDDR to increase its reliance on Civil Service employees and retirees, and expand mentoring to help address midlevel experience gaps overseas. To expand the limited number of Civil Service employees filling overseas positions, State began a pilot program to offer additional opportunities for overseas assignments and eased requirements for conversions from Civil Service to Foreign Service. State also hires retirees on a limited basis to help fill gaps overseas. In addition, State began a pilot program offering a workshop with mentoring for first-time supervisors overseas. However, State's Five Year Workforce Plan does not include a specific strategy to guide efforts to address midlevel gaps.

State Has Taken Steps to Expand the Use of Civil Service Employees in Midlevel Overseas Positions

State's first QDDR, released in 2010, highlighted the goal of expanding the use of Civil Service employees to help close the midlevel experience gap. The QDDR noted that State has a base of Civil Service employees with significant experience and called for increasing opportunities for Civil Service employees to fill overseas Foreign Service assignments and increasing the number of Civil Service conversions to the Foreign Service. A February 2011 report by the American Academy of Diplomacy and the Stimson Center also recommended expanded use of Civil

Service employees to fill midlevel gaps.[14] As a first step, State recently conducted a survey of its Civil Service employees and found a high level of interest in serving overseas. About 75 percent of respondents expressed interest in serving in some type of overseas assignment in their careers and about 25 percent expressed interest in eventually converting to Foreign Service, according to State officials.

The extent to which State currently draws on its pool of Civil Service employees for overseas assignments is limited. From fiscal years 2009 through 2011, State placed 159 Civil Service employees in overseas Foreign Service positions in temporary assignments. These are known as "Limited Non-Career Appointments" (LNA). According to State officials, many of these assignments fill midlevel positions. State's human capital rules enable Civil Service employees (and other non-Foreign Service employees) to serve as LNAs, normally for up to 5 years.[15] However, the duration of these assignments typically ranges from 1 to 3 years, according to State officials.

Many of these LNA assignments are for positions that the department has identified as "hard-to-fill," meaning they lack sufficient qualified bidders from among the ranks of the Foreign Service. In an announcement to the department each May, State identifies hard-to-fill positions for which Civil Service employees may apply.[16] Most of these positions are at the midlevel. State listed 36 hard-to-fill positions in 2009, 74 in 2010, and 55 in 2011. Other common types of overseas LNA assignments for Civil Service employees include positions in AIP countries, developmental opportunities, and positions requiring specific expertise.

State Human Resources Bureau officials we met with identified several key challenges to assigning Civil Service employees to overseas assignments. In particular, these assignments can create gaps in the

---

[14]Henry L. Stimson Center, American Foreign Service Association, and American Academy of Diplomacy, *Forging a 21st-Century Diplomatic Service for the United States through Professional Education and Training* (Washington, D.C.: February 2011).

[15]Rules governing LNAs are covered in the Foreign Affairs Manual (3 FAM 2290) and federal law (22 U.S.C. §§ 3943, 3949).

[16]These positions continue to be available for Foreign Service employees to bid on. Local eligible family members may also bid on these positions and would have priority over Washington-based Civil Service employees.

positions Civil Service employees leave behind. Affected bureaus must guarantee that applicants will be placed into permanent Civil Service positions within the same bureau when they return from their overseas assignments. This requirement creates some reluctance on the part of bureaus to approve applications for overseas assignments, according to State officials. In addition, department officials noted that Civil Service employees have concerns about losing future opportunities for desirable Civil Service positions while serving overseas. Another challenge is that State cannot always identify a sufficient number of qualified Civil Service employees to apply for the overseas vacancies it seeks to fill. State officials noted that hard-to-fill positions are typically not in the more desirable locations, which they said contributes to limited interest among qualified Civil Servants. In addition, it can often be difficult to match Civil Service employees' qualifications with the needs of the open positions.

The Human Resources Bureau began a pilot program in November 2011 to expand opportunities for Civil Service employees to serve in overseas positions. It was intended to support goals highlighted in the QDDR to enhance career development for midlevel Civil Service employees and ease Foreign Service midlevel staffing gaps. The department identified 11 overseas positions at various posts to which qualified Civil Service employees could apply. Most of these assignments are for midlevel positions. The assignments in the pilot differ from the hard-to-fill assignments in two key ways. First, these are not positions that Foreign Service bidders initially passed over. Second, the re-employment rules are more flexible, according to Human Resources Bureau officials; affected bureaus do not have to hold a position for the Civil Service employees who participate in the pilot. Instead, returning Civil Service employees can be placed in a bureau different from the one they vacated.

According to State officials, the department has agreed with AFSA to limit the total to about 20 assignments at any one time during the pilot to ensure that the program does not limit career development opportunities for Foreign Service employees.[17] The officials noted that Foreign Service employees operate in an "up-or-out" personnel system, which requires them to have sufficient experience and responsibilities to progress in their

---

[17]State plans to offer additional overseas assignment opportunities to Civil Service employees on a rolling basis to keep the total number of these assignments within 20 at any one time. State indicated in April 2012 that the program would soon offer five additional positions.

careers. In addition, efforts to increase the number of Civil Service assignments to Foreign Service positions must be consistent with State's human capital rules, which state that the department's goal is to fill Foreign Service positions with Foreign Service employees except under special circumstances.[18] The overseas positions in the pilot program continue to be designated as Foreign Service positions and can be filled by Foreign Service employees after the Civil Service employees complete their assignments.

Human Resources Bureau officials stated that they expect this pilot program to help the department assess its ability to identify overseas positions that match the skills and experience of potential Civil Service applicants. It will also identify potential staffing impacts on affected bureaus and posts, as well as career development needs of the Foreign Service. However, according to the officials, the department has not finalized plans for evaluating the results of the pilot program. They also noted that it will be more than 2 years before the first set of assignments is completed and they can begin to survey participants and stakeholders to assess results of the pilot program.

State's QDDR also included a goal of expanding opportunities for Civil Service employees to convert to the Foreign Service to help fill experience gaps overseas. The QDDR stated that, while all State personnel can apply to enter the Foreign Service through the traditional selection process, it is in the department's interest to offer more and quicker pathways for qualified and interested Civil Service employees to join the Foreign Service. However, State's Foreign Service Conversion Program has strict eligibility requirements, which limit the number of conversions. The program's application and review process resulted in only three Civil Service applicants recommended for conversion in 2010 and four in 2011.

State only opens positions for conversion that it projects to be in deficit or otherwise approved by the Director General and lists them in an annual

---

[18]This goal is articulated in the Foreign Affairs Manual (3 FAM 2293). In addition, 22 U.S.C. § 3982 states that the Secretary of State shall assure that positions designated as Foreign Service positions normally shall be filled by the assignment of members of the Foreign Service to those positions.

GAO-12-721 Foreign Service Workforce Gaps

cable that it circulates throughout the department.[19] The department convenes a review panel to confirm that applicants meet minimum qualifications, which include 24 months in Foreign Service positions abroad out of the previous 6 years; and 30 months of service—domestically or overseas—in the desired skill code in the previous 6 years. The panel then determines if applicants have the skills and experience necessary to perform successfully in the positions for which they are applying. Applicants offered an opportunity to convert based on the panel review must then submit a proctored writing sample, which must earn a passing grade from the Foreign Service Board of Examiners to be recommended for conversion.[20]

According to Human Resources Bureau officials, in 2011, State identified 88 Foreign Service generalist positions as open for conversion from Civil Service, as well as Foreign Service generalist and specialist. Twenty-six Civil Service applicants applied. Ultimately, the process resulted in seven applicants given the opportunity to convert and four of the seven passing the writing test requirement. Table 1 shows the number of applicants who qualified at key stages in the process in 2010 and 2011.

Table 1: Civil Service Conversions to Foreign Service Generalist Positions in 2010 and 2011

Year	Number of applicants who met minimum qualifications	Number of applicants offered opportunity to convert	Number of applicants passing writing test requirement
2010	30	8	3
2011	26	7	4[a]

Source: State.

[a]Number includes two applicants not required to take the writing test because they previously passed the Foreign Service Oral Assessment.

Human Resources Bureau officials noted that in 2011, the department sought to ease the qualification requirements somewhat, including reducing the number of months served overseas from 30 months to 24

---

[19]This cable articulates the rules governing its Foreign Service Conversion Program. Foreign Service specialists may also apply for conversion to open generalist positions and generalists may apply to convert to a different generalist job category.

[20]Applicants are not required to take the writing exam if they have previously passed the Foreign Service Oral Assessment.

GAO-12-721 Foreign Service Workforce Gaps

months; however, the number of qualified applicants actually dropped from 30 in 2010 to 26 in 2011. Beginning in 2012, the assessment process will include a structured interview, along with the writing test, to give candidates an additional means of demonstrating their skills and competencies.

State Hires Retirees for Both Full-Time and Temporary Overseas Assignments, but Their Use Is Limited

Retirees can fill key roles at overseas posts, bringing with them a high level of skills and experience, according to State officials. The department has limited authority to hire retirees for full-time positions and also for temporary assignments. State's QDDR noted that the department should draw on its pool of retirees to help address its overseas midlevel gap. In addition, the Stimson Center and American Academy of Diplomacy report also recommended that State increase reliance on retirees.

State hires retired Foreign Service and Civil Service employees to work full-time with waivers from federal dual compensation rules, under certain circumstances, to help fill workforce gaps overseas. In calendar year 2011, State approved 57 dual compensation waivers for 35 Foreign Service retirees and 22 Civil Service retirees for overseas assignments. Federal law requires that payment of a retiree's annuity terminates on the date of re-employment except under circumstances in which State has the authority to grant a dual compensation waiver.[21] These circumstances include staffing needs in AIP countries and emergency situations involving a direct threat to life or property, or other unusual circumstances.

State officials stated that they would make greater use of dual compensation waivers to draw from the pool of retirees to fill experience gaps if their legal authority were expanded. However, other than State's

---

[21]22 U.S.C. § 4064 specifies dual compensation restrictions related to hiring Foreign Service retirees and gives authority to the Secretary of State to waive these restrictions under certain circumstances. 5 U.S.C. §§ 8344 and 8468 provide similar restrictions related to hiring Civil Service retirees and gives authority to the Director of the Office of Personnel Management (OPM) to waive these restrictions at the request of the head of an Executive agency, on a case-by-case basis. OPM has delegated this waiver authority to State every year since 2001 in response to the September 11, 2001 attacks. The National Defense Authorization Act (NDAA) of 2010 also provided the Secretary of State (along with other specified Federal Agency heads) with authority to grant a limited number of dual compensation waivers to Civil Service retirees, if the head of the agency determines that reemployment is necessary to "fulfill functions critical to the mission of the agency" or to "respond to an emergency involving a direct threat to life or property."

Office of Inspector General, the department has not formally sought expanded congressional authority to offer waivers to hire Foreign Service retirees.[22] The Office of Inspector General is seeking separate congressional authority for additional dual compensation waivers to help meet its staffing needs, including filling positions at its overseas posts in hardship locations, such as Amman, Jordan; Cairo, Egypt; and Kabul, Afghanistan.

State hires many more Foreign Service retirees for temporary, part-time work than it does for full-time assignments. These retirees work on a "When Actually Employed" schedule and are commonly referred to as "WAEs." WAEs do not fill vacant positions overseas but are an important means of addressing workforce gaps, according to State officials. For example, posts often rely on WAEs to fill staffing gaps during summer rotations of Foreign Service employees, according to State officials. Officials also noted that WAEs can be particularly helpful when short-term needs arise requiring special skills and expertise, such as helping posts prepare for a presidential visit or evacuating an embassy during a crisis. Newer staff also can benefit from the experience and expertise that WAEs share during their assignments.

Federal rules, and high salary and travel costs, limit the extent to which State uses WAEs. State bureaus typically hire them for short assignments of 1 to 3 months. Federal law enables Foreign Service retirees to earn a salary while continuing to receive their retirement annuity as long as their total earnings do not exceed the greater of an amount equal to the basic pay they earned when they retired or the highest annual rate of basic pay for full-time employment in the position for which they have been re-employed.[23] This limits the amount of time they can work in a calendar year. According to State officials, WAEs also have a cap of 1,040 hours of employment per calendar year.[24] In addition to rules in federal statute that limit their use, WAEs are also a relatively expensive option because of their high salaries and travel costs, according to State officials from the

---

[22]OPM is responsible for policy related to Civil Service annuitants.

[23]22 U.S.C. § 4064(b).

[24]State employs these WAEs under their authority to make a temporary limited appointment. As an exception to the general time limits for such a position, State fills the position with WAEs provided that each appointment does not exceed 1,040 hours in a calendar year. 5 C.F.R. § 316.401.

geographic bureaus and the Bureau of Consular Affairs—the primary users of WAEs. Table 2 shows the number of WAE appointments these bureaus used in 2011 and the average duration of each appointment. Individual bureaus maintain their own lists of retirees and hire them as WAEs from their own budgets. State has no initiatives currently under way to expand its use of WAEs.

Table 2: WAE Appointments, by Bureau, in Fiscal Year 2011

Bureau	Number of WAEs	Average duration
African Affairs	86	3.4 months
European and Eurasian Affairs	25	2.3 months
East Asian and Pacific Affairs	16	2.1 months
Near Eastern Affairs	52	2.5 months
South and Central Asian Affairs	28	2.2 months
Western Hemisphere Affairs	19	1.8 months
Consular Affairs	119	1.4 months

Source: GAO analysis of State data.

Note: Number of WAE appointments includes instances in which the same individual had more than one appointment.

State Began a Pilot Training Workshop for Overseas First-Time Supervisors to Help Mitigate Midlevel Experience Gaps

As part of its effort to address Foreign Service experience gaps, State's QDDR included the goal of expanding existing mentoring programs and piloting a new mentoring program for first-time supervisors. State currently offers mentoring for entry-level Foreign Service employees and situational mentoring, which offers advice for any State employee on a specific activity or issue. In addition, State officials noted that less experienced Foreign Service employees are increasingly being asked to fill supervisory roles earlier in their careers than in the past, which raises the need for targeting this group for additional mentoring.

In September 2011, the Human Resources Bureau began a pilot program offering training workshops designed to improve the skills of first-time supervisors overseas. Mentoring, both at and following the training, is a key component of the pilot workshops, according to bureau officials. The pilot involved two 5-day workshops—one in Fort Lauderdale, Florida, and another in Frankfurt, Germany, delivered to a total of 49 first-time supervisors from three of the department's geographic regions. The workshops focused on performance management and basic leadership skills. Retirees served as class mentors and established relationships with the participants at the sessions. The mentors are expected to follow up with the attendees for 1 year, with the possibility to travel to their overseas posts, if warranted.

According to Human Resources Bureau officials, the program included follow-up surveys of attendees and their supervisors to assess the usefulness of the workshops in improving participants' management style and skills. The officials noted that the response among the participants and their supervisors has been positive. State plans to conduct two more sessions in September 2012 for first-time supervisors from the department's other three geographic regions. State officials noted that the pilot needs to be completed before they can determine the effectiveness of the program. A potential constraint is the cost of sending officers to these workshops.

State Has Not Developed a Strategy to Address Midlevel Gaps

Although State has undertaken efforts to carry out QDDR goals to address midlevel gaps, the department has not developed a strategic approach to guide these efforts. We have found in prior work that developing a strategy to address staffing gaps and evaluating its success contribute to effective workforce plans.[25] State's Five Year Workforce Plan outlines its human capital strategies; however, the plan lacks a specific strategy for addressing midlevel experience gaps. In our prior work, we developed a workforce planning model that suggests that, when considering a strategy to address workforce gaps, agencies consider the full range of flexibilities available under current authorities, as well as flexibilities that might require additional legislation before they can be adopted. State's efforts to draw on its pool of retirees and Civil Service employees to fill midlevel gaps are examples of the use of such flexibilities; however, it is not clear that State has developed a strategy to take full advantage of its authority to use them.

In addition, our workforce planning model suggests that, to evaluate human capital strategies, agencies develop performance measures that can be used to gauge progress toward reaching human capital goals. State's Five Year Workforce Plan does not indicate how it will evaluate efforts under way to address midlevel gaps. State plans to assess its two

---

[25]GAO, *Human Capital: Key Principles for Effective Strategic Workforce Planning,* GAO-04-39 (Washington, D.C.: December 2003).

pilot programs, but it has not developed performance measures to gauge the potential impact of these efforts on midlevel gaps.

Conclusions

State faces persistent Foreign Service experience gaps at overseas posts, particularly at the midlevels, and these gaps put its diplomatic readiness at risk. State has traditionally relied on hiring new Foreign Service employees to fill overseas gaps and significantly increased hiring in fiscal years 2009 and 2010. However, those new hires will not be eligible for promotion to the midlevels until at least fiscal year 2014 and projections for future annual hiring increases have been reduced due to budgetary constraints. As a result, State likely will continue to face staffing and experience gaps for the foreseeable future. These gaps will continue to affect diplomatic readiness as positions remain unfilled or are staffed by Foreign Service employees whose experience does not match the position requirements. In the meantime, State has taken steps to implement goals highlighted in the QDDR to address midlevel overseas gaps, including developing pilot programs for increasing the use of Civil Service employees overseas and providing new workshops with mentoring for first-time supervisors overseas. Although these efforts are currently small in relation to the size of the overall gaps, their impact and the extent to which they can be expanded in the future have yet to be analyzed by State and are, therefore, unclear. Since State has not developed a specific strategy for addressing midlevel gaps, it can neither fully assess the success of its efforts to close these gaps nor determine the optimal course of action for enhancing diplomatic readiness.

Recommendation for Executive Action

To help guide State's efforts to address midlevel gaps in the Foreign Service, we recommend that the Secretary of State direct the Bureau of Human Resources to update its Five Year Workforce Plan to include a strategy to address these gaps and a plan to evaluate the success of this strategy.

Agency Comments

We provided a draft of this report to State for comment. In its written comments, reproduced in appendix III, State agreed with our recommendation. State also provided technical comments, which we incorporated throughout the report, as appropriate.

As agreed with your office, unless you publicly announce the contents of this report earlier, we plan no further distribution until 30 days from the report's date. At that time, we will send copies to the Secretary of State and other interested congressional committees. In addition, the report is available at no charge on the GAO website at http://www.gao.gov.

If you or your staff have any questions about this report, please contact me at (202) 512-8980 or courtsm@gao.gov. Contact points for our Offices of Congressional Relations and Public Affairs may be found on the last page of this report. GAO staff who made key contributions to this report are listed in appendix IV.

Sincerely yours,

Michael J. Courts
Acting Director
International Affairs and Trade

Appendix I: Objectives, Scope, and Methodology

In this report, we assess: (1) the extent to which the Department of State's (State) overseas midlevel Foreign Service experience gaps have changed since 2008 and (2) State's efforts to address these gaps.

To assess the extent of the State's overseas midlevel Foreign Service experience gaps and how these gaps have changed since 2008, we

- reviewed GAO and State Office of Inspector General reports, as well as State workforce planning and budget documents and its Diplomacy 3.0 initiative;

- collected and analyzed staffing data on all overseas Foreign Service positions from State's Global Employees Management System (GEMS) as of September 30, 2008, and October 31, 2011;[1] and

- interviewed officials in State's Bureau of Human Resources, Bureau of Consular Affairs, and six regional bureaus regarding overseas experience gaps.

To determine the extent of overseas Foreign Service experience gaps, we analyzed State staffing data. We compared the number of positions that were vacant, filled with upstretch assignments, and filled at grade or higher with the total number of authorized overseas positions. We did not validate whether the total number of authorized overseas positions was appropriate or met State's needs. We calculated total vacancy and upstretch rates across all overseas Foreign Service positions for both the 2008 and 2011 data. We also calculated vacancy and upstretch rates for both data sets by each of the following characteristics: level (i.e., entry-, mid-, or senior-level); type (i.e., generalist or specialist); and function (e.g., consular or information management). For 2011 data only, we supplemented the GEMS data with additional State data on hardship differentials and embassy and nonembassy rankings from State's Overseas Staffing Models and also calculated vacancy and upstretch rates by each of these characteristics.

---

[1]We obtained position data as of October 31, 2011, because, according to State officials, most employees moving on to their next assignments have arrived at their new posts by that time and most promotions have taken effect. However, State officials noted that some positions may appear vacant in GEMS because incoming incumbents have not yet arrived at their new posts. We used data as of the end of fiscal year 2008 obtained for a prior GAO report at that time for similar reasons.

To calculate vacancy rates, we divided the total number of positions by
the number of vacant positions. To calculate upstretch rates, we divided
the total number of positions by the number of upstretch assignments. We
considered any assignment in which the grade of incumbent was at least
one grade lower than that of the position as an upstretch assignment, with
one exception: According to State officials, tenured Foreign Service
generalists with a position grade of 04 are not considered in an upstretch
assignment if they encumber a position with an 03 grade because
tenured 04 grade officers are expected to fill positions with an 03 grade, if
possible. We, therefore, did not consider tenured 04 grade officers to be
in an upstretch assignment when they filled positions graded as 03. We
considered senior-level positions at the Career Minister, Minister
Counselor, and Counselor level to be of a comparable grade and,
therefore, did not consider officers with any of these grades to be in an
upstretch assignment. According to State officials, the department does
not consider any employee in an entry-level position to be in an upstretch
assignment. However, for the purposes of our analysis, we defined any
assignment in which the position's grade is higher than the incumbent's
grade to be an upstretch assignment. Therefore, because State assigns
different grades to positions within the entry levels, we considered entry-
level assignments where a position's grade was higher than the
employee's grade to be upstretch assignments.

We eliminated a small number of positions from our analysis of each data
set because we could not clearly or completely identify where the
positions were located. We also eliminated 57 Security Protective
Specialist positions from the 2011 data because, according to State
officials, it was a new job category and was not intended for permanent
Foreign Service Officers, but rather employees hired under short-term
limited noncareer appointments. In total, we did not use 88 positions, or
about 1 percent of the total, from the September 30, 2008, data and 207
positions, or about 2 percent of the total, from the October 31, 2011, data,
which we determined did not substantially affect our findings.

We also conducted an analysis of the likelihood of overseas positions
being vacant or filled through upstretch assignments based on the various
characteristics described above. For a detailed discussion of the
methodology and results of that analysis, see appendix II.

We obtained staffing and position data from State's GEMS database.
Since we have previously checked the reliability of this database, we
inquired if State had made any major changes to the database since our
2009 report. State indicated that it had not made major changes to the

system. We also tested the data for completeness, confirmed the general
accuracy of the data with select overseas posts, and interviewed
knowledgeable officials from the Office of Resource Management and
Organizational Analysis concerning the reliability of the data. Data from
Afghanistan, Iraq, and Pakistan (AIP) posts often show higher vacancy
rates than actually exist at the post; however, it does so because State
relies heavily on short-term assignments to fill positions in these
locations. These short-term assignments do not show up in GEMS, and
the position, therefore, appears vacant. Positions in GEMS represent a
need for full-time, permanent Foreign Service employees, and, therefore,
we determined that the GEMS data accurately reflect State's ability to fill
positions in these locations with full-time, permanent Foreign Service
employees. Additionally, because State often pulls staff from other
overseas assignments to fill short-term temporary assignments in AIP
countries, the vacancy rate for all overseas positions is most accurately
captured when all posts are included. Therefore, based on our analysis of
the data and discussions with the officials, we determined the data to be
sufficiently reliable for our purposes. However, when referring specifically
to vacancy rates in AIP countries, we reference other State sources,
which include positions filled through both permanent and temporary
assignments.

To assess State's approach to addressing midlevel Foreign Service gaps
through expanded use of Civil Service employees, retirees, and
mentoring, we

- reviewed GAO and State Office of Inspector General reports;

- reviewed relevant State documents, such as State's Quadrennial
  Diplomacy and Development Review (QDDR), State's Five Year
  Workforce Plan, and the Bureau of Human Resources' Bureau
  Strategic and Resource Plan;

- reviewed federal laws, policies, and regulations governing Limited
  Non-Career Appointments (LNA) of Civil Service Employees,
  conversion from Civil Service to Foreign Service, and hiring of retired
  Foreign Service and Civil Service annuitants; and

- interviewed officials in State's Bureau of Human Resources, Bureau
  of Consular Affairs, and six regional bureaus, the American Foreign
  Service Association, and the American Academy of Diplomacy
  regarding overseas experience gaps and the potential to address
  gaps through the use of Civil Service, retirees, and mentoring.

We collected and analyzed data on the retirees hired with dual compensation waivers in calendar year 2011. We also collected and analyzed data on the use of retirees hired for temporary, short-term assignments, referred to as "When Actually Employed" (WAE) in fiscal year 2011 from each of the six regional bureaus and the Bureau of Consular Affairs. We analyzed that data based on the number of assignments made, rather than the number of retirees used, as State officials noted that some individuals may be used in multiple assignments. In addition, we collected and analyzed data on overseas LNA assignments of Civil Service employees for fiscal years 2009 through 2011 from State's Bureau of Human Resources. Because these assignments may be for multiple years, the number of assignments made does not necessarily reflect the number of Civil Service employees serving overseas at any one time. We also collected data on the results of State's 2010 and 2011 Foreign Service Conversion Program, including the number of positions available, the number of Civil Service applicants, and the number offered conversion opportunities. We found the data on the use of retirees and Civil Service employees overseas to be sufficiently reliable for our purposes. We focused only on efforts related to expanding the use of Civil Service employees, retirees, and mentoring because they were highlighted in State's QDDR as key means of addressing overseas midlevel gaps.

To supplement our other analysis, we met with officials in Amman, Jordan; Kyiv, Ukraine; New Delhi, India; Santo Domingo, Dominican Republic; and Sao Paulo and Brasilia, Brazil, to obtain firsthand knowledge about experience gaps and use of Civil Service, retirees, and mentoring at overseas posts. We conducted this work in conjunction with a separate study on visa fraud and selected posts that met criteria established for both studies, including the size of staffing gaps and the level of visa fraud.

We conducted this performance audit from June 2011 to June 2012 in accordance with generally accepted government auditing standards. Those standards require that we plan and perform the audit to obtain sufficient, appropriate evidence to provide a reasonable basis for our findings and conclusions based on our audit objectives. We believe that the evidence obtained provides a reasonable basis for our findings and conclusions based on our audit objectives.

Appendix II: Analysis of Factors Associated with Vacancies and Upstretch Assignments

In this appendix, we describe the methods we used to determine what factors were related to whether positions at the State Department were vacant as of October 2011 and those that were filled by upstretch assignments—employees whose grades were lower than the grades of the positions filled. We first considered a set of bivariate tables (or two-way cross-classifications) that indicated what percentage of positions were filled and left vacant, across categories that reflected

- the level of the position (entry level, midlevel, and upper level);

- the hardship category associated with the position (least, medium, and greatest);[1]

- the type of position (generalist versus specialist);

- the Overseas Staffing Model ranking and type of post where the position was located (embassies ranked 1 or 2 were combined and contrasted with embassies ranked 3, 3+, 4, 5, 5+, and nonembassies of any rank);[2]

- region (Africa, East Asia and the Pacific, Europe and Eurasia, Near East, South and Central Asia, and Western Hemisphere); and

- whether the position was in Afghanistan, Iraq, or Pakistan (collectively referred to as AIP) or elsewhere (non-AIP).

We then calculated odds and odds ratios from the observed percentages in these tables, which allowed us to summarize the differences in the likelihoods of positions remaining vacant across the different types of positions, and conducted a series of bivariate and multivariate regression analyses to estimate the significance of those differences when we considered each of these six factors one at a time, when we considered

---

[1]"Least hardship" included posts with a hardship differential of 10 percent or less; "medium hardship" included posts with hardship differentials between 15 percent and 20 percent; and "greatest hardship" included posts with hardship differentials of 25 percent or more.

[2]State's Overseas Staffing Model assigns embassies a ranking of 1 through 5+, based on the requirements of the embassy. These levels are closely associated with the department's foreign policy priorities, with higher numbers representing higher foreign policy priorities. Because nonembassies are provided functional rankings that are not necessarily associated with a location's priority, we included them as a separate group.

five of them simultaneously (all but AIP), and finally when we considered all six of them simultaneously. Finally, we conducted parallel analyses that involved looking at the same types of two-way tables and estimating the same bivariate and multivariate regression models to determine, among those positions that were filled, whether they were filled by upstretch assignments as opposed to officers at or above grade. We describe these analyses as follows.

The first three columns of numbers in table 3 show the percentage of positions that were filled and vacant across the categories of the six factors just described, and the numbers of positions in each category on which those percentages were based. A slightly smaller percentage of upper-level positions than entry-level positions were vacant (12.6 percent versus 14.9 percent), and a much larger percentage of the positions in the greatest hardship category (20.5 percent) than in the least hardship category (10.4 percent) were left vacant. While there was little difference between generalist positions and specialist positions, there were some sizable differences across different posts with different rankings, with positions in the highest-ranked embassies (20.9 percent) and in nonembassies (16.4 percent) showing the highest percentages of vacancies. Higher percentages of positions in the Near East (22.3 percent) and South and Central Asia (24.2 percent) were left vacant compared with other regions, and positions in AIP countries were much more likely to be vacant than those in non-AIP locations (39.5 percent vs. 11.4 percent).[3]

---

[3]State relies heavily on temporary assignments—which do not show up as filled, in State's personnel database—to fill positions in AIP. Additionally, State continuously fills positions in AIP throughout the year, so vacancy rates may differ greatly at different points in time. According to State data as of February 2012, over one-quarter (27 percent) of the positions at AIP posts that were filled were filled with temporary assignments.

Table 3: Percentages of Positions with Different Characteristics That Were Filled and Vacant, and Odds and Odds Ratios Indicating the Differences between Categories

Position characteristic	Percentage of positions		Number of positions	Odds on vacant	Odds ratios
	Filled	Vacant			
Position level					
Entry level	85.1	14.9	2,330	0.18	1.04
Midlevel	85.6	14.4	5,727	0.17	REF
Upper level	87.4	12.6	999	0.14	0.86
Missing	50.0	50.0	2		
Hardship category					
Least hardship	89.6	10.4	3,993	0.12	REF
Medium hardship	86.4	13.6	2,280	0.16	1.36
Greatest hardship	79.5	20.5	2,785	0.26	2.22
Type of Position					
Generalist	86.0	14.0	5,173	0.16	REF
Specialist	85.2	14.8	3,885	0.17	1.07
Post type/ranking					
Embassy 1 or 2	89.2	10.8	742	0.12	0.46
Embassy 3	87.1	12.9	1,407	0.15	0.56
Embassy 3+	90.0	10.0	1,718	0.11	0.42
Embassy 4	89.8	10.2	509	0.11	0.43
Embassy 5	90.7	9.3	814	0.10	0.39
Embassy 5+	79.1	20.9	2,074	0.26	REF
Nonembassy	83.6	16.4	1,621	0.20	0.74
Missing	79.2	20.8	173		
Region					
Africa	91.0	9.0	1,182	0.10	0.78
East Asia and Pacific	87.7	12.3	1,446	0.14	1.10
Europe	88.8	11.2	2,231	0.13	0.99
Near East	77.7	22.3	1,347	0.29	2.25
South and Central Asia	75.8	24.2	1,085	0.32	2.51
Western Hemisphere	88.7	11.3	1,767	0.13	REF
AIP					
Non-AIP	88.6	11.4	8,121	0.13	REF
AIP	60.5	39.5	937	0.65	5.07
Total	**85.7**	**14.3**	**9,058**	**0.17**	

Source: GAO analysis of State Department Global Employee Management System Data on overseas positions, as of October, 31 2011.

Note: For each characteristic, we use one category as the referent category (REF). The resulting odds ratios can be interpreted in relation to that category. For example, midlevel positions are the referent category for position level. The odds ratios for entry-level positions indicate that those positions had slightly higher odds of remaining vacant than midlevel positions, by a factor of 1.04, while upper-level positions had slightly lower odds than midlevel positions of remaining vacant, by a factor of 0.86.

In the last two columns of table 3, we show the odds on positions being vacant, and odds ratios that indicate the proportional differences in those odds across the different categories of positions. The odds on positions being vacant are calculated by dividing the percentage of positions that are vacant by the percentages that are filled, within each of the categories of the different positions. For entry-level positions, for example, we divide 14.9 by 85.1 to obtain 0.18, which indicates that 0.18 positions were vacant for every one that was filled or, alternatively, that 18 were vacant for every 100 that were filled. Similar calculations for midlevel and upper-level positions yield slightly smaller odds (equal to 0.17 and 0.14, respectively), and odds that differ quite substantially across other categories of positions, such as those with the greatest hardship (0.26) versus least hardship (0.12), and those in South and Central Asia (0.32) versus the Western Hemisphere (0.13).

The odds ratios in the final column of table 3 indicate the proportional differences in the odds of positions remaining vacant across the categories of each of the position characteristics. To estimate these odds ratios, we choose one category of each characteristic as the referent category (indicated by REF in the table), and divide the odds for the other categories by the odds for the referent category. For example, we chose midlevel positions as the referent category with respect to position level, divided 0.18 and 0.14 by 0.17, and the resultant odds ratios indicate that entry-level positions had slightly higher odds of remaining vacant than midlevel positions, by a factor of 1.04, while upper-level positions had slightly lower odds than midlevel positions of remaining vacant, by a factor of 0.86. Similar calculations using the different categories of the other position characteristics reveal that positions with greatest and medium hardship were more likely to be vacant than those with least hardship, by factors of 2.22 and 1.36, respectively, while specialist positions had only slightly higher odds than generalist positions of remaining vacant, by a factor of 1.07. Also, all of the lower-ranked embassies had roughly half or less than half the odds of embassies ranked 5+ of remaining vacant, and nonembassies had odds that were lower than the highest-ranked embassies by a factor of 0.74. Finally, positions in Africa had lower odds on remaining vacant than positions in the Western Hemisphere (by a factor of 0.78), positions in East Asia and the Pacific and in Europe had odds that were very similar, and positions in the Near East and South and Central Asia had higher odds on remaining vacant than positions in the Western Hemisphere, by factors of

2.25 and 2.51, respectively. As the final multivariate model in table 4 shows, some of these regional differences were because AIP countries were more than five times as likely as those in other areas to be vacant.[4]

Odds ratios identical to those just discussed, apart from slight rounding error, are shown in the first column of table 4. The unadjusted odds ratios in the first column of table 4, however, were estimated using a series of bivariate logistic regression models, which allow us to test whether the different contrasts specified by the various odds ratios are significantly different than 1. Significant odds ratios are bolded in the table, and we can see the unadjusted ratios reflecting the differences in the odds on positions remaining vacant across position level categories and between generalist and specialist positions are not significant; in addition, the differences between positions in the East Asia and Pacific region, Europe, and the Western hemisphere are not significant. All of the other unadjusted (or bivariate) odds ratios are significant, though our judgment about both the size and significance of these differences is only tentative since they are unadjusted and fail to take into account that the different position characteristics—for example, hardship level and region—may be related to one another and, as such, the estimated unadjusted effect of one characteristic may be accounted for by the effect of another.

Table 4: Unadjusted and Adjusted Odds Ratios Indicating the Differences in the Odds on Positions Being Vacant between Positions with Various Characteristics

| | | Adjusted odds ratios | |
| | | Without AIP | With AIP |
Categories contrasted	Unadjusted odds ratios	indicator	indicator
Entry-level vs. midlevel positions	1.04	**1.22**	**1.36**
Upper-level vs. midlevel positions	0.86	0.87	0.88
Medium hardship vs. least hardship	**1.36**	**1.21**	**1.22**
Greatest hardship vs. least hardship	**2.22**	**2.25**	**1.44**
Specialist vs. generalist positions	1.07	1.06	1.06
Africa vs. Western Hemisphere	**0.78**	**0.54**	**0.67**
East Asia and Pacific vs. Western Hemisphere	1.11	0.85	1.09

[4]State relies heavily on temporary assignments—which do not show up as filled, in State's personnel database—to fill positions in AIP. Additionally, State continuously fills positions in AIP throughout the year, so vacancy rates may differ greatly at different points in time. According to State data as of February 2012, over one-quarter (27 percent) of the positions at AIP posts that were filled were filled with temporary assignments.

Categories contrasted	Unadjusted odds ratios	Adjusted odds ratios	
		Without AIP indicator	With AIP indicator
Europe vs. Western Hemisphere	0.99	1.00	1.08
Near East vs. Western Hemisphere	**2.26**	**1.54**	1.23
South Central Asia vs. Western Hemisphere	**2.52**	**1.28**	0.90
Rank 1 or 2 embassy vs. Rank 5+ embassy	**0.46**	**0.61**	1.00
Rank 3 embassy vs. Rank 5+ embassy	**0.56**	**0.62**	1.14
Rank 3+ embassy vs. Rank 5+ embassy	**0.42**	**0.49**	0.85
Rank 4 embassy vs. Rank 5+ embassy	**0.43**	**0.62**	0.87
Rank 5 embassy vs. Rank 5+ embassy	**0.39**	**0.57**	0.87
Nonembassy vs. Rank 5+ embassy	**0.74**	0.87	1.20
AIP vs. non-AIP positions	**5.07**		**4.12**

Source: GAO analysis of State Department Global Employee Management System data on overseas positions, as of October 31, 2011.

Note: Bolding indicates odds ratios that are statistically significant at the 0.05 level.

In the middle column of the table, we show the results of re-estimating these odds ratios using a multivariate model that estimates the effects on positions remaining vacant of all of these factors simultaneously, except for the AIP indicator. Under this model, most of the effects remain significant, though the difference between nonembassy positions and embassy positions is diminished and insignificant, and the difference between entry-level and midlevel positions increases and becomes significant.

In the final column, we show the results of re-estimating these odds ratios using a multivariate model that estimates the effects of all six factors simultaneously, including the war zone indicator. As can be seen, the adjusted difference between AIP and non-AIP positions is sizable (OR = 4.12), and allowing for that difference accounts for all of the differences between embassies of different ranks and nonembassies, and most of the differences between regions (the exception being the difference between positions in Africa and the Western Hemisphere). In summary, when all factors are considered simultaneously and the associations between characteristics are taken into account, the differences that are statistically significant are as follows:

- entry-level positions have higher odds of remaining vacant than midlevel positions, by a factor of 1.36;

- positions in the greatest hardship and medium hardship categories are more likely than those in the least hardship category to remain vacant, by factors of 1.44 and 1.22, respectively;

- positions in Africa are less likely to remain vacant than those in the Western hemisphere, by a factor of 0.67; and

- AIP positions are slightly more than four times as likely to remain vacant as non-AIP positions.

Table 5 shows similar bivariate results in which these six characteristics are cross-classified by whether the position was filled by employees whose grades were lower than the grades of the position they filled, and table 6 shows the significant and insignificant odds ratios from bivariate and multivariate models used to estimate the effects of those characteristics on this outcome. While there is no need to labor over a discussion of all of the percentages and odds and odds ratios in table 5, which show the unadjusted and sometimes sizable differences across categories of position in the likelihood of being filled by a lower-graded employee, they are there for the reader to see. Our bottom-line findings, from the multivariate model coefficients in the final column of table 6 in which all position characteristics are considered simultaneously and the effect of each is estimated net of the others, are as follows:

- Upper-level positions are more than twice as likely as midlevel positions to be filled by upstretch assignments.

- Positions in the greatest hardship and medium hardship categories are more likely than those in the least hardship category to be filled by lower-level employees, by factors of 1.81 and 1.47, respectively.

- Specialist positions are less likely than generalist positions to be filled by employees whose grades are lower than the positions, by a factor of 0.75.

- Positions in East Asia and the Pacific and Europe are less likely to be filled by upstretch assignments than those in the Western hemisphere, by factors of 0.80 and 0.72, respectively.

- The lowest-ranked embassies (ranks 1 and 2) are only about half as likely as the embassies ranked 5+ to be filled by upstretch assignments, while embassies with other ranks and nonembassies are not significantly different from embassies ranked 5+.

- AIP positions are half as likely to be filled by upstretch assignments as non-AIP positions.

Table 5: Percentages of Positions with Different Characteristics That Were Filled by Employees Below Grade Level Versus at or above Grade Level, and Odds and Odds Ratios Indicating the Differences between Them

Position characteristic	Percentage of positions filled by employees		Number of positions	Odds on below	Odds ratios
	At or above grade level	Below grade level			
Position level					
Low level	84.1	15.9	1,983	0.19	1.16
Mid level	86.0	14.0	4,905	0.16	REF
Upper level	73.1	26.9	873	0.37	2.26
Missing	100.0	0.0	1		
Hardship category					
Least hardship	86.8	13.2	3,578	0.15	REF
Medium hardship	81.9	18.1	1,969	0.22	1.45
Greatest hardship	81.6	18.4	2,215	0.23	1.48
Type of position					
Generalist	82.8	17.2	4,451	0.21	REF
Specialist	85.7	14.3	3,311	0.17	0.80
Post type/ranking					
Embassy 1 or 2	89.4	10.6	662	0.12	0.64
Embassy 3	84.2	15.8	1,226	0.19	1.02
Embassy 3+	82.9	17.1	1,546	0.21	1.12
Embassy 4	84.5	15.5	457	0.18	0.99
Embassy 5	79.0	21.0	738	0.27	1.44
Embassy 5+	84.4	15.6	1,641	0.18	REF
Nonembassy	84.9	15.1	1,355	0.18	0.96
Missing	84.7	15.3	137		
Region					
Africa	80.9	19.1	1,076	0.24	1.10
East Asia and Pacific	84.5	15.5	1,268	0.18	0.85
Europe	87.4	12.6	1,981	0.14	0.67
Near East	83.6	16.4	1,047	0.20	0.91
South and Central Asia	83.3	16.7	822	0.20	0.93
Western Hemisphere	82.3	17.7	1,568	0.22	REF
AIP					
Non-AIP	83.9	16.1	7,195	0.19	REF
AIP	86.1	13.9	567	0.16	0.84
Total	**84.1**	**15.9**	**7,762**		

Source: GAO analysis of State Department Global Employee Management System data on overseas positions, as of October, 31 2011.

Note: For each characteristic, we use one category as the referent category (REF). The resulting odds ratios within that characteristic can be interpreted in relation to that category

Table 6: Unadjusted and Adjusted Odds Ratios Indicating the Differences in the Odds on Positions Being Filled with Below-Grade Employees between Positions with Various Characteristics

| | | Adjusted odds ratios | |
Categories contrasted	Unadjusted odds ratios	Without AIP indicator	With AIP indicator
Entry-level vs. midlevel positions	**1.17**	1.04	1.02
Upper-level vs. midlevel positions	**2.27**	**2.24**	**2.23**
Medium hardship vs. least Hardship	**1.45**	**1.48**	**1.47**
Greatest hardship vs. least hardship	**1.47**	**1.62**	**1.81**
Specialist vs. generalist positions	**0.80**	**0.75**	**0.75**
Africa vs. Western Hemisphere	1.10	1.07	1.02
East Asia and Pacific vs. Western Hemisphere	0.85	0.84	**0.80**
Europe vs. Western Hemisphere	**0.67**	**0.74**	**0.72**
Near East vs. Western Hemisphere	0.92	0.88	0.93
South Central Asia vs. Western Hemisphere	0.93	**0.77**	0.86
Rank 1 or 2 embassy vs. rank 5+ embassy	**0.64**	**0.56**	**0.49**
Rank 3 embassy vs. rank 5+ embassy	1.02	0.93	0.79
Rank 3+ embassy vs. rank 5+ embassy	1.12	1.12	0.97
Rank 4 embassy vs. rank 5+ embassy	1.00	1.13	1.03
Rank 5 embassy vs. rank 5+ embassy	**1.44**	**1.41**	1.25
Nonembassy vs. rank 5+ embassy	0.96	1.05	0.95
AIP vs. non-AIP positions	0.84		**0.57**

Source: GAO analysis of State Department Global Employee Management System data on overseas positions, as of October, 31 2011.

Note: Bolding indicates odds ratios that are statistically significant at the 0.05 level.

Appendix III: Comments from the Department of State

United States Department of State

Chief Financial Officer

Washington, D.C. 20520

Dr. Loren Yager
Managing Director
International Affairs and Trade
Government Accountability Office
441 G Street, N.W.
Washington, D.C. 20548-0001

JUN - 4 2012

Dear Dr. Yager:

We appreciate the opportunity to review your draft report, "DEPARTMENT OF STATE: Foreign Service Staffing Gaps Persist Despite Significant Increases in Hiring" GAO Job Code 320849.

The enclosed Department of State comments are provided for incorporation with this letter as an appendix to the final report.

If you have any questions concerning this response, please contact Bert Curtis, HR Policy Specialist, Bureau of Human Resources at (202) 647-2655.

Sincerely,

James L. Millette

cc: GAO – Michael Courts
        DGHR– Linda Thomas-Greenfield
        State/OIG – Evelyn Klemstine

Department of State Comments on GAO Draft Report

DEPARTMENT OF STATE: Foreign Service Staffing Gaps Persist Despite Significant Increases in Hiring
(GAO-12-721, GAO Code 320849)

Thank you for the opportunity to comment on your draft report entitled, *"Department of State: Foreign Service Staffing Gaps Persist Despite Significant Increases in Hiring."*

The Department appreciates the description of the Department of State's staffing challenges. We believe that GAO has written a comprehensive review of the efforts undertaken by the Department as well as the new challenges that have arisen since the 2008 GAO engagement regarding the staffing of hardship posts and the subsequent publication, "Additional Steps Needed to Address Staffing and Experience Gaps."

GAO recommended that the Secretary of State direct the Bureau of Human Resources to update its primary workforce planning document to include a strategy to address Foreign Service staffing gaps and a plan to evaluate its success. We agree with GAO that such a strategy could be an effective tool to guide State's efforts to address mid-level gaps in the Foreign Service. While we believe that our Five Year Workforce and Leadership Succession Plan, updated and published annually, contains all of the strategy elements necessary to address mid-level staffing gaps, they are not all assembled in one section/chapter as the plan is not designed to focus on this one workforce issue. The current Plan, 2012-16, is in its final stages of publication.

As we move into the development of the 2013 – 2017 update of the Plan, we will consolidate the strategies and evaluative components regarding the mid-level staffing and experience gaps into a more comprehensive and focused section/chapter of the Five-Year Plan.

Appendix IV: GAO Contact and Staff Acknowledgments

GAO Contact	Michael J. Courts, (202) 512-8980 or courtsm@gao.gov
Staff Acknowledgments	In addition to the contact named above, Anthony Moran, Assistant Director; Howard Cott; Kara Marshall; Grant Mallie; Doug Sloane; Martin De Alteriis; Karen Deans; and Grace Lui provided significant contributions to the work.

GAO's Mission	The Government Accountability Office, the audit, evaluation, and investigative arm of Congress, exists to support Congress in meeting its constitutional responsibilities and to help improve the performance and accountability of the federal government for the American people. GAO examines the use of public funds; evaluates federal programs and policies; and provides analyses, recommendations, and other assistance to help Congress make informed oversight, policy, and funding decisions. GAO's commitment to good government is reflected in its core values of accountability, integrity, and reliability.
Obtaining Copies of GAO Reports and Testimony	The fastest and easiest way to obtain copies of GAO documents at no cost is through GAO's website (www.gao.gov). Each weekday afternoon, GAO posts on its website newly released reports, testimony, and correspondence. To have GAO e-mail you a list of newly posted products, go to www.gao.gov and select "E-mail Updates."
Order by Phone	The price of each GAO publication reflects GAO's actual cost of production and distribution and depends on the number of pages in the publication and whether the publication is printed in color or black and white. Pricing and ordering information is posted on GAO's website, http://www.gao.gov/ordering.htm. Place orders by calling (202) 512-6000, toll free (866) 801-7077, or TDD (202) 512-2537. Orders may be paid for using American Express, Discover Card, MasterCard, Visa, check, or money order. Call for additional information.
Connect with GAO	Connect with GAO on Facebook, Flickr, Twitter, and YouTube. Subscribe to our RSS Feeds or E-mail Updates. Listen to our Podcasts. Visit GAO on the web at www.gao.gov.
To Report Fraud, Waste, and Abuse in Federal Programs	Contact: Website: www.gao.gov/fraudnet/fraudnet.htm E-mail: fraudnet@gao.gov Automated answering system: (800) 424-5454 or (202) 512-7470
Congressional Relations	Katherine Siggerud, Managing Director, siggerudk@gao.gov, (202) 512-4400, U.S. Government Accountability Office, 441 G Street NW, Room 7125, Washington, DC 20548
Public Affairs	Chuck Young, Managing Director, youngc1@gao.gov, (202) 512-4800 U.S. Government Accountability Office, 441 G Street NW, Room 7149 Washington, DC 20548